just do good work

a simple guide towards the evolution of us
psychotherapists after Erickson

Rob McNeilly

ISBN: 0995358133
ISBN-13: 978-0-9953581-3-3

just do good work: a simple guide towards the evolution of us psychotherapists after Erickson /Rob McNeilly

Cover Photo: "The Kiss" a marble sculpture by Auguste Rodin was made in 1903 and this third replica is in Ny Carlsberg Glyptotek, Copenhagen, Denmark. Photographed by Rob McNeilly March 2010

Tandava Press
www.tandavapress.com
Tandavapress@gmail.com

Printed in the United States of America

This book is offered as a humble gesture of appreciation of my teachers, particularly Milton Erickson, and also to my family however close or distant.

It is my sincere wish that it might contribute to our reclaiming the sacred in our work so we can again honour the mystery that we are all part of.

DISCLAIMER

This book is not based on science, statistics or evidence. There are no techniques, no recommendations, no suggestions.

It is a result of my experience of emphasising the importance of our mood of expectancy and a firm persistence in listening to each individual person, respecting their legitimacy, to create a context where healing can happen naturally and with a minimum of suffering.

There is a saying that we stand on the shoulders of giants, which can be comforting, but do we need to bear the burden of having giants stand on our shoulders?

If we can honour each person, and ourselves, we can have the possibility of standing on our own feet, and even learning to dance...

"To make the impossible possible, the possible easy,
and the easy elegant"
Moshe Feldenkrais

"In the beginner's mind there are many possibilities,
but in the expert's there are few."
Shunryu Suzuki

"Many scholars have made the Buddha's teaching complicated and difficult to understand. But the Buddha said things very simply and did not get caught up in words. So, if a teaching is too complicated, it is not the sound of the Buddha."
Thich Nhat Hanh

"Gentlemen, I have a confession to make. Half of what we have taught you is in error and furthermore, we cannot tell you which half it is."
Sir William Osler

Contents

FOREWORD

BY SCOTT D MILLER PH.D.

I was 24 years old when I entered graduate school in psychology. It was an exciting time and I was prepared to learn the keys to helping others suffering from mental, emotional, and behavioral difficulties. Some four years later, I graduated. Sitting opposite the people I was now qualified to help, I often felt plagued by the feeling that I must have missed that one crucial day in school when they had taught everyone how it all worked — the secret to successful psychotherapy.

Much of what I learned seemed so generic: listen, start where the person is at, accept them as they are, and so on. I went to workshops, read books, even moved across the country in my effort to better understand how to be effective. I was soon overwhelmed by both the scope and complexity of theories and methods available for describing and doing therapy. Eventually, I lucked into a position with a team of talented thinkers and practitioners working together to develop their own treatment approach. The name doesn't matter. I finally had what I'd long been searching for: direction and clarity.

Thanks to the team and the countless hours spent watching and performing the approach, I eventually mastered the method. I could do it in my sleep. No matter the person or presenting problem, I was confident I could help. I *knew* what to do.

As a group, we invited two researchers from outside the agency to follow up with our clients and evaluate the efficacy of model we had developed. At the conclusion of their study, they returned, asking whether we wanted to hear the good or the bad news first? Unable to imagine what the latter might be, we opted to hear the former.

"What you've developed here," they told us, "works." This came as no surprise to any members of our team — after all, we had met with the clients ourselves, knew we were effective. When asked about the bad news, they continued, "No more effective than any other approach that's been developed over the last 100 years." It was a blow, to say the least. More important, it served to undermine my long held belief that healing was a matter of figuring out the right method to apply to the problem at hand.

Decades of subsequent research have confirmed my disillusionment, at the same time documenting that the single best predictor of treatment outcome is client engagement. Said another way, whatever we do that facilitates participation, increases the chance of a positive result. Here, the key, it turns out, is being with people in a way that makes them want to be who they are with you!

Like other simple ideas, this one is easier said than done.

Rather than diagnosing problems and applying protocols, learning to "Just do Good Work" — as Rob McNeilly's guide advises — requires thoughtful and ongoing, planning and reflection. Read this brief treatise in an hour — which one can easily do — and almost certainly, you will get little from it. Take one paragraph or page at a time, and it will transform your development as a helper and healer.

Scott D. Miller, Ph.D
Director, International Center for Clinical Excellence

The Short Version

Accept each client as a legitimate other.

This does not require approval or agreement, but simply recognising that at this moment, they are who they are.

Listen to each client for what they want.

This does not require that we go along with what they want, but simply explore possible learning opportunities with them.

Maintain a personal mood of expectancy.

This does not require being optimistic or expecting a positive outcome, but simply being open to the possibility that at any moment, for no good reason, a useful change can happen.

When in doubt, ask.

Some Background

My father was part of a humble family of nine children in Motherwell, now a suburb of Glasgow, Scotland. He had four brothers, two of whom were tipplers and two were Plymouth Brethren preachers. He liked simple pleasures and was nearly totally lacking in ambition. I like my whisky, and my wife still has to remind me from time to time to "get off the pulpit."

My mother was part of a humble family of four children in Geelong near Melbourne, Australia. She was very ambitious for her children and instilled in us the importance of hard work and self-reliance.

When I first met Milton Erickson, towards the end of his life, I was an enthusiastic convert to the "Church of Erickson." He was the way and the truth and the life. More than a third of a century later I continue to be inspired by what I learnt from my time with him, and I have also come to recognise that he was a human being, with human limitations, which only adds to my appreciation of what he was pointing to. Confucius said, "When the wise man points at the Moon, the idiot looks at the finger."

For me, his approach has not been fully appreciated, and although many writers have attempted to extract components of what they saw, they missed his essence. Instead of the contemporary obsession with explaining and quantifying, he invited a practical approach - one based on observing and responding. This avoids the argy bargy between different theories and honours the uniqueness of each individual.

This book is inspired by him and invites a simple and radically different approach to therapy and learning - one which invites direct experience through observing, and development of effectiveness by increasing our sensitivities rather than requiring theories and techniques.

The idea of writing this book was sparked by Scott Miller's comments in the 2013 Evolution of Psychotherapy Conference, where he claimed that there has been no evolution of psychotherapy and called for an evolution of *psychotherapists*.

My first response was to call for a *devolution* of psychotherapy. The return to the Taoist "uncarved block," to honour the fundamental human conversations that happen when therapy is at its best.

This led on to an interest in exploring the self of the therapist - how we can be as human beings to contribute to the therapy process - in particular creating a mood of expectancy or possibility and honouring the legitimacy of each client.

Finally, I saw that both can be important - we can return to the fundamentals of human beings and also explore how we as therapists can develop our skills in relating with our clients through listening, learning, being flexible and restoring genuine trust.

These are the central themes of what follows.

Milton Erickson continues to be the core source of my exploration. Other influences are Martin Heidegger's "clearing," Fernando Flores' "sensitivities" and my personal learning with Fernando Flores, Humberto Maturana, Julio Olalla, Rafael Echeverria, indirectly from Werner Erhard, the perspectives of Zen and the Stoics, the whimsy of Nasrudin, and the timeless benison of Lao Tzu.

The substance of the book is a result of my work as a therapist over the last 40 years and teaching workshops around the globe over the last 35 years, and more recently, through the extraordinary opportunity of online workshops. I continue to be amazed by the experience of live video conversations with a group of people from Greenland, Spain, France, Belgium, UK, USA, and of course, Australia.

It has been my passion to find human ways of working therapeutically to expand possibilities through respect and humble exploration in ways that are simple without being simplistic, creating learning that is easy without trivialising, and methods of extending our skills without making this into a chore. All this through a melding of widely divergent, even unlikely sources towards some integration, by exploring the common ground in their fundamental assumptions.

Milton Erickson invited us to "Just do good work," hence the title of this book, but typical of the man, gave no specific steps on how to achieve this. He gave us a clue when he said that the three most important skills for us to learn are to observe, to observe, and to observe.

Joseph Campbell's recommendation to "Follow your bliss" led to a later quip that he should have said "Follow your blisters" as there is work to do… And again, we are left without clear steps about how to find our bliss and where we should aim to develop blisters.

Let's not overlook serendipity. The universe can be so generous in giving us opportunities, which appear as if by chance, and which we overlook at a great cost and all too often, with a feeling of regret.

Albert Einstein spoke of "combinatory play," as the ability to connect the seemingly unconnected by cross-pollinating questions and evoking creativity. This resonates with me as I have been impressed with the way most of my important learning about therapy have not come from therapy, but from seemingly unconnected fields, including music, dancing, personal development programmes and gardening.

What follows are some of my reflections on the "whats" and the "hows" so we could explore and learn towards effectiveness in our work.

I am not presuming to be definitive, but rather to offer some ideas, to share some experiences, and most importantly, to invite your own exploration and application of these ideas, and to then find someone to support your learning - a colleague, an experienced supervisor, mentor, or coach - someone solidly grounded in these perennial areas of learning.

So, as you read this, I invite you to be willing to discover what might already be familiar, and perhaps see it even more clearly; to notice aspects of your work where you would be willing to explore even further and learn more; to find ways of making your learning enjoyable; and to be open to uncovering the common everydayness in the complex as well as the wonder of the common everyday.

Let the learning continue …

Section 1

Foundations

The Gift of Expectancy

One Sunday afternoon a little girl asked her father to take her to the shop so she could have an ice-cream. The father, expecting that the shop would most likely be shut, was reluctant, but when the daughter said, wide-eyed, and cute, "You never know!" the father found himself taking her there, and the shop WAS open. They went, the shop was open and the daughter had her ice-cream. The source of her ice-cream was her mood of expectancy, not the shop, and certainly not from her father's mood.

All problems occur in a mood of resignation. Clients don't come saying that they have a problem and they know that at any moment, it is going to vanish! They always know and often say that they don't see any way out of the dilemma, no possibility of solving it, and this mood of resignation is a fundamental component of any problem.

What is missing then is *the possibility* of a solution, but stating that will only add to the stuckness, implying that not only is this person defective, since they have the problem, but also stupid since they can't see something that is obvious to us. The only way that a possibility has any chance of becoming available, visible, and so accessible, is if we can invite a different *mood* - one of possibility, of expectancy.

We know that moods are infectious, and unless we take care of our own mood, we are in danger of "catching" a client's mood of resignation. If we begin with our mood of expectancy, this can inoculate us against catching the client's unhelpful mood and set up the possibility of them catching our expectancy.

One of the most useful ways of putting ourselves into a mood of expectancy is simply to be open to the possibility that something useful can happen at any time for no apparent reason.

We all benefit.

Expectancy is not being optimistic. It is not thinking positive. Both of these are an expression of expectations - we expect that something good will happen. In a mood of expectancy, we are anticipating the *possibility* of something good happening, not the actuality, so if it doesn't happen, we can be peaceful, not disappointed.

Expectancy, for me, is an open-ended *attitude,* where we don't assume or require a particular outcome, rather we are open to a wide range of possibilities.

I like to think of expectations as something quite specific that we have about some future event. We expect the sun to rise, we expect a plane to take off. For me, this is a function of me that I impose on another person or event. A teacher might say to a student, "I expect you to do better next time," and this comes from the teacher, and can so easily be felt like a criticism or a negation by the student.

Expectations are a universal cause of suffering, and the Stoic, Seneca, reminded us that if we want to be happy, we should lower our expectations. I would add that if we want to increase our satisfaction, we should increase our expectancy.

Paul Leslie has written about hoodoo in his delightful book "Low Country Shamanism" as a practice of putting a curse, or in hoodoo "putting the root" on someone. Root doctors can also remove a curse to free the sufferer from the problem caused by the curse, or having the root put on someone else. This practice is an example of the power of expectations and is social, and not likely to be effective for anyone who doesn't share those cultural expectations.

Some parents, teachers, and medical experts use their authority to issue a label, diagnosis or prognosis without owning the cruel limitations that these pronouncements can cause. Children can be labeled as "bad" or "dumb." Clients can be labeled as incurably suffering from PTSD, OCD or psychosis. These people in authority would be horrified to be associated with something as "primitive" as hoodoo, and some therapists might not like to be associated with Root Doctors, but we can all learn, and as well as being careful about any unintentional limitations we could impose, we can explore ways to help remove such limitations and create more possibilities.

In some approaches to therapy, the therapist has expectations of the client based on a particular theory of therapy. If the client doesn't meet those expectations, there is talk of resistance, secondary gain, or lack of readiness.

After my time with Erickson, I have come to appreciate the wonderful gift that our expectancy can offer a stuck client. I'll illustrate this with two cases that Erickson told me about.

A woman rang Erickson saying that a number of her friends had been to see him with good results, and she had a problem that she thought Erickson could help her with. When he offered an appointment, she said she was too embarrassed to see him. When he offered a phone session, she said she was too embarrassed to even speak about her problem in the phone. She asked for permission to park her car in his driveway over the next 3 Tuesday evenings. He said that would be fine, and noticed that there was an unfamiliar car in his driveway on those evenings. After the third evening, she rang, reported that she felt so much better and was very grateful for his help. He never met her!

A suicidally depressed client had to drive interstate with her work, and Erickson gave her the task of watching out for a bright flash of colour on her trip. Instead of her habitual internal ruminations, she was looking out for this bright flash of colour. She was looking in a mood of expectancy, and when she returned, she reported that it was a bright red parrot that flew across the road!

In both these cases, it wasn't Erickson expectations that were important - it was the client's expectancy, embodied then invited by Erickson, that created the possibility for the change to happen.

Also, there is a beautiful little word with big possibilities – "YET." "I haven't improved" then becomes "You haven't improved... yet." What a transformation! What a distillation of expectancy!

Some possible hows for you to explore:

Notice any time you have a mood of expectancy - looking forward to seeing your partner, children, family, your dog, a cup of tea - and gently be aware of it. The more you notice this, the more familiar it will become, and the easier it will be to access.

Notice when anyone - family member, client, character on TV - is expectant. Be willing to be surprised how often you will see this.

Any time you are with a client and you feel the heaviness of resignation, recall the experience and/or intentionally place your body in the positions of expectancy.

Notice any time you feel disappointed. What were your expectations? What's different when you notice this?

Here are some questions for you...

When you experience this mood of expectancy, give some attention to your body.

How are your eyebrows - up, neutral or down?

How are your eyes - wide open, neutral or partly closed?

How is your mouth - open, closed?

And the corners of your mouth - up, down?

How's your jaw - loose, tight?

Your shoulders - up, down, back, forward?

Your chest - loose, tight?

Your breathing - shallow, deep?

Your stomach - tight, loose?

Your hands - clenched, open?

Anything else?

Again, the more familiar you become with your body in expectancy, the easier it will be to find it when you want.

And questions to play with clients...

What's it like when the problem isn't there or isn't so bad?

What will the first sign be that the solution is happening?

Who will be the first person to notice some relief in you?

How will you know that this difficulty is completely resolved?

When you tell me that you don't need to see me anymore, what will be - different for you - in your thinking, your feelings, your actions?

Add "yet" to any stuckness. "You haven't noticed any im-provement *YET*."

ACCEPTING

A tourist became lost in Ireland and went into a pub to ask for directions. He opened a map and showed the publican where he started and where he wanted to go. After considerable thought, the publican replied "Well, I wouldn't be starting from here."

Probably the best known quote from Lao Tzu's Tao Te Ching is #64, "A journey of a thousand li begins with the first step." There are other translations - "The journey of a thousand li begins with the ground beneath your feet," "Reality begins where you are," "This is it," and my very favourite, "Knowing nothing needs to be done is the place from where we begin."

Erickson spoke of a man in a psychiatric hospital who would only say, "I shouldn't be here." He replied and asked the staff to also reply with, "But you are here!" The man eventually heard the reply and said, "Oh, my goodness! What do I need to do to get out of here?" He had to get "here" before there was any possibility of getting out of "here."

If our car gets bogged, the temptation is to spin the wheels, which of course, will only make things worse. The first step is to realise that the car is bogged so that then, and only then, we can begin to explore ways out of the bog.

When I went into my waiting room to meet the first client one Thursday morning, I was hit by the stench of stale cigarette smoke. The man looked like he needed a good wash and I thought, "Is this how I want to spend my life?" I was polite, hopefully hiding my disgust, as he told me he that he wanted help to stop smoking. As we talked, he spoke of his fascination with philosophy, and Martin Heidegger in particular, and I slowly began to appreciate this man as more than his stench. As I accepted him, we connected, the session progressed, and he was happy with the outcome. The main impediment was my slowness to accept him, and when this was put aside, all was well.

Some possible hows for you to explore:

Notice and own any judgements you make.

Put these judgements aside for the moment, without giving them up.

Imagine that you are the other person looking out through their eyes, with their history of life experiences.

VALIDATING

We can feel agony when we see someone suffering and unable to resolve it. They are suffering and we are in agony. It's natural to want to relieve their suffering so that our agony is relieved. It's tempting, and understandable, but just not helpful. If we try, the other will suffer more - the original suffering persists and there is the additional experience of being misunderstood, trivialised, disrespected.

A man had been to many therapists before he saw Erickson. Erickson began the session by saying, "You've seen a lot of therapists and none of them have been able to help you. You must already be losing faith in my ability to help you." This was the beginning of the possibility of some relief.

Solution Focused Therapy was criticised some years back for being too focused on finding a solution, and was nick-named "Solution Forced Therapy" where we are going to force you to have a solution whether you want it or not! Anyone working in a solution approach can feel reluctant to speak about the suffering, the stuckness some clients have, for fear that this might increase them. It goes with the territory. However counterintuitive it may seem, validation of someone's stuckness and suffering can be a necessary first step towards creating the possibility of resolution. It can be miraculous.

I recall a man shouting down the phone at me one evening because he blamed me that his wife was wanting a divorce. My natural reflex was to defend myself and justify my position since I didn't know she was going to ask for a divorce. Instead, I was able to say, "You sound very upset," and he replied, "Of course I'm upset. We've been married for 30 years and I had no warning about this. Can I have an appointment tomorrow to discuss this?" His rage evaporated with this simple experience of being validated.

Whenever we are stuck, or a client is stuck, there is a simple rule of thumb - down tools and validate.

Although this can seem weird and against the optimistic mood of possibility creation, it provides a solid foundation for any possibilities to emerge. The worry that by acknowledging the suffering we might worsen it, in my experience and that of others I have spoken to, doesn't support this worry - actually the opposite.

If we observe a client's response to their stuckness, we can observe their frustration, sadness, hopelessness, fear about their stuckness and then articulate this - "I can imagine that you are frustrated, sad, feeling hopeless or frightened [whatever we have observed]." I have witness people weep with relief of someone acknowledging the severity of their pain, the massiveness of their suffering instead of disrespectfully attempting to resolve it.

Some possible hows for you to explore:

When someone has already seen multiple therapists, observe their mood. Are they frustrated, resigned, doubtful, suspicious? ... Even ask them how they feel. Then say, "I'm not surprised that you're feeling ... If I'd been through what you've been though, I'd expect to be feeling … also." It's important that this comment be sincere so the client doesn't feel trivialised or disrespected.

Then observe any change, and don't make any attempt to start any changes until you can see that the client has been adequately validated.

Then, and only then, begin your helping.

And, any time the progress stalls, down tools again, and validate, again!

SECTION 2

CREATING THE THERAPEUTIC RELATIONSHIP

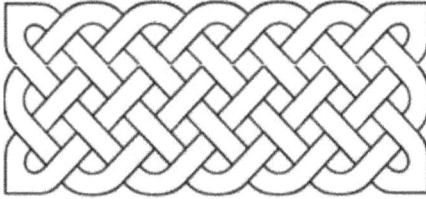

When we connect with another person, listening can happen, which contributes to the connection. When we are learning together with a client, we connect and listen more effectively. When there is genuine trust, connection, learning and listening happens, etc. Each contributes to all aspects of the therapeutic relationship.

Our exploration of the components individually is artificial, and can also lead to a synergistic wholeness.

CONNECTING

"Because we are, I am"
Xhosa saying

Connecting with another human being, animal, plant, landscape is not an intellectual experience. It is sacred - an experience of the soul. When we connect, we can feel an emotion of being touched or moved and can bring tears. This is not trivial. It is a fundamental human experience.

One of the joys of our work is witnessing a client connecting with their solution, their joy, their future, their partner. It touches us, nurtures us and we can know that this is why we do what we do. It's more than a job, a position, a collection of techniques and skills. It's a calling - a sacred calling.

We humans are connecting beings. We need air, water, food, and connections or we wither and die.

How often do we hear a client speak of their feelings of isolation, loneliness, emptiness?

So much of our western emotional suffering is a function of lack of connections. We lock ourselves in behind high fences to exclude others. We fight and go to war by disconnecting with the other.

If there is a war, the first propaganda move is to disconnect with the enemy by casting them as different and less than human. Only then is it possible for a human being to kill them.

On the first Christmas Eve of The First World War, soldiers from both armies discovered they were singing the same Christmas carols. They began to throw gifts across no-man's land and finally came out and exchanged badges and other items. When the fighting was due to begin the following day, it was not possible. The soldiers had connected with the "enemy" and were unable to attempt to kill them. I spoke to a man whose grandfather was there, and he said his grandfather and the rest of those British soldiers had to be sent home. There was a serious risk of peace breaking out until the officers in charge managed to prevent it.

There is a saying, "You don't know another person until you've walked a mile in their shoes." A comic added that if you still don't like them, then at least you're a mile away and you have an extra pair of shoes.

I have found that connecting is a skill we can learn - therapists and clients.

A father and son wanted help to get past their conflict. I asked them to stand facing each other with their left foot forward and their right foot back and get a firm grip on the other's hands, then to begin a sawing motion, back and forth, looking into each other's eyes. It was a high-energy experience for both of them, but they were coordinating their connection without conflict. They agreed to play with this and even do this exercise if either of them felt a conflict coming on. Their problem dissipated.

I asked an arguing couple to stand facing each other and let their fingertips be in gentle touch with their partner's fingertips, and then to move their left hand in a random direction so that each had to keep their right fingertips in contact to maintain the connection. They were both quietly enjoying the gentle connection and were able to learn to translate this into their everyday living together.

Maturana claims that love is the fundamental social human emotion and is created by accepting another as they are and granting them legitimacy to live in the world beside us. When we do this, we generate an experience of connecting with them, and so the possibility of them connecting with us.

Some possible hows for you to explore:

When you are with a client, listening to them, imagine yourself in their situation - the sights, sounds, smells, feelings as they describe them.

Match your breathing, blinking and body posture with the client.

LEARNING TO LEARN

Erickson said, "All our life we are learning," "All problems are learnt limitations," and in Haley's Advanced Techniques, "In the process of living, the price of survival is eternal vigilance and the willingness to learn. The sooner one becomes aware of realities and the sooner one adjusts to them, the quicker is the process of adjustment and the happier the experience of living."

Any problem-solving approach requires that we focus on what's wrong that needs fixing. By contrast, a solution approach assumes that what's missing for each individual client is some disconnection from a resource that they have got out of touch with, forgotten, or have not yet learnt.

This approach transforms the therapeutic relationship from one where the expert therapist has the knowledge and the power to one where client and therapist can work together, as two human beings, to facilitate the resource connection or learning, and predictably aids the healing experience.

Learning creates all of our responses, and so, all of our experiences, both problematic and satisfying. Learning can also create a different future, one which is preferred.

Learning implies a process. Too often, we and/or our clients expect an instant and permanent resolution of a problem.

When we learn any new skill, we make a beginning, make mistakes, correct them, improve, and although some learnings happen immediately and are permanent, others come and go. We achieve some competence and lose it, needing to review, practice more, be patient... By associating problem resolution with learning, everyone is relieved from the pressure of having to make a sudden jump to competence. Clients have permission to take their time, find their own way, make their own variations, get it wrong so they can correct it, and we have permission to be patient and supportive.

Michel Tomas was a wonderful language teacher and has left behind a collection of language lessons where he insists that there is no need to practice, do homework, or memorise anything. All that is required is to listen, repeat the words, and enjoy the experience. In one Spanish lesson, he claimed that any English word that ended in '-tion' was identical in Spanish, except it became '-cion', and with that small insight, any student suddenly had learnt several thousand Spanish words! He also emphasises the importance of enjoying the process, through effortless repetition. How different from the usual method of laboriously repeating words and phrases, which is boring and abstract.

How Do We Learn?

A girl of five wanted to learn to ride her two-wheeler bike, and over two days, she fell off, got back on, fell off, got back on and after those two days, she was covered with bruises, but she could ride her bike. When her younger brother was ready, he avoided even trying until one day after his parents had given up on him ever learning, he got on his bike and rode it - no falling off, no bruises. They both learnt to ride, and each in their own time, and in their own way.

Everyone has their own learning style. Some like to read, others to listen, others to watch, or jump in the deep end or learn by playing.

We can approach any problem as an opportunity to learn. My friend, Ben Furman, has written a series of publications about "Kids Skills" where he explores with the family what skills are to be learnt by this child, who can help, how can the achievement be celebrated?

Learning by immersion in a direct experience is then possible, with recurrent practice in a safe environment where principles are embodied by the teacher and learnt by the student without needing to explain the theory behind what they are learning.

This allows the development of "sensitivities" though a cycle of observing and responding to clients' responses to our responses in a recurrent dancing conversation that allows the therapist to be in the client's "clearing," "zone," "groove," "flow," instead of our own. It avoids the need for reflection, which requires a therapist and client to leave the dance, come up with a plan to improve techniques, and only then return to the dance to try the refinement. This recurrent movement on and off the dancefloor requires withdrawal from the client's clearing, zone, groove, flow, and although it is a legitimate way, it's not the only way.

Learning also gives us access to solid confidence, which is an issue for any therapist. New therapists struggle to become confident. Seasoned therapist can be so confident that they become arrogant. Genuine confidence, then, as distinct from the pretense of confidence, is a function of competence and the way to competence is learning, for all levels of experience and continuing throughout our life.

There is nothing more scary than someone who is confident while being incompetent. It can be terrifying teaching someone to drive when they asked how soon they could find a road where they could drive fast, and just as relieving when someone asks for our patience because they were only going to drive slowly to begin with.

Our contemporary attitude to learning is based on understanding, theorising, memorising, and application of what is learnt, so to become confident, we would need to read books, go to workshops, study at universities. The problem is that there is never enough knowledge to cover all situations. There's always another textbook, paper, or workshop, so becoming confident becomes a topless mountain.

If instead, we begin to explore skills that can lead to effectiveness in our work, then we are drawn to learning, to listen, be flexible, restore trust, to generate a mood of expectancy... and develop competencies in these skills, we can create a healing therapeutic relationship. We can then give up having to pretend to have "the knowledge" and instead, find ourselves experiencing genuine, solid confidence.

Erickson said, "You can always be totally confident that your client has all the resource needed to resolve their problem," inviting us to learn to be confident in recognising the client's abilities, not obsessing about ours.

Obviously, becoming more effective in our work requires learning, but does it have to be difficult or complicated or hard work?

It can be a function of learning to observe, with a narrow focus on the present situation, and a wide focus on all our embodied past learning, being flexible so our response can evolve.

Some possible hows for you to explore:

How do you learn? Not only therapy, but other areas as well. How did you learn to walk as a child? How did you learn to read and write, to ride a bicycle, swim, drive a car? Do you like to read, watch demonstrations, attend workshops...? What methods have been most useful for your learning? What others might you be interested to explore?

We can ask a client about how they learn things. It can be particularly helpful to ask about something they enjoy and how they learnt that? This can transform the pressure to solve the problem or get rid of it into a process. Learning happens over time, comes and goes, until it's solidly a part of us. This can also invite the possibility of learning instead of suffering or trying, as well as a reminder that they have already learnt many things, so this can be just one more.

THE GENTLE ART OF LISTENING

Nan-in, a Japanese master during the Meiji era [1869-1912], received a university professor who came to enquire about Zen.

Nan-in served tea. He poured his visitor's cup full, and then kept on pouring.

The professor watched the overflow until he no longer could control himself. "It is overfull. No more will go in!"

"Like this cup," Nan-in said, "you are full of your own opinions and speculations. How can I show you Zen unless you first empty your cup?"

How Can We Listen… ?

how can we listen… ?
we can listen
all too well
to our own thoughts-self
all too easily loud
to our own self-aware
how can we listen… ?
how can we listen… ?
through our deafening
head-machinations
through our half-remembered
half-forgotten petty-worries
how can we listen… ?
how can we listen… ?

to the silent screams

through others' teeth-clenched

to the silent smile

through others' mouth corners-upturned

to the silent laugh

of others' eyes corner-smiling

to their soul mouth-flapping

against our mumbled ears

how can we listen... ?

Listening is recognised as an essential part of effective counselling, but what is listening? How can we listen effectively?

As human beings, we have all experienced the healing that follows someone really listening to us - to our joys and our suffering. We have also had the experience of someone not listening, often resulting in a sadness or being misunderstood, or trivialised. As therapists, we have also witnessed a client's response when they feel listened to... and when they don't!

Listening to and being listened to is not related to hearing or understanding. It is an experience which touches our soul, where at a deep human level, there is acceptance and legitimacy. Through listening, we create connections between human beings.

Listening both requires a mood of empathy and also creates it. As we listen to another, we create a mood of empathy, and when we are empathic, we can listen. Either can lead so the other can follow, or they can show up together. We all value empathy and enjoy the connecting experience it allows. The word "empathy" is relatively new, only created in 1909 from the German *einfühlung*, literally "feeling into," which was used to describe the imaginative act of projecting oneself into a work of art in an effort to understand why art moves us. Empathy, then, invites us to "feel into" another and be moved by the experience of connecting.

Listening engages the listener and listenee. When we are in the experience together, it's not surprising to discover the importance of empathy and engagement in creating a trusting therapeutic relationship and so worth our serious attention as a skill to develop.

Rafael Echeverria of Newfield Consulting wrote, "Listening is not a simple phenomenon. Many factors intervene in the way we listen and in the way we are listened to. However, from our old understanding of language, it is difficult to grasp what listening is really about. We claim that in a world with the diversity of ours, listening has become a major issue in ensuring effective communication. Today we must learn to listen better to be able to live together in harmony. This is necessary when we relate as couples, in communities, at work, in the marketplace, etc. It is valuable to develop a new understanding of what listening is about. This will open for us the possibility of competence in effective listening."

Erickson knew about listening instinctively when he said that the three most important skills for us to do good work are... "To observe; to observe; and... to observe."

I have noticed that even though I value listening, and hold it as an essential component of doing good work, sometimes I fail dismally.

Some of what gets in my way are listening to my own thoughts, expectations, certainties, judgements so there's no room for the other.

How can we get ourselves out of the way so listening to the other becomes possible?

Some actions I have found to be helpful are:
- Simply shifting my focus from me to the client by observing them
- Putting my arrogance aside to make room for some humility
- Remembering to accept the other as a legitimate other
- Being inspired by others [examples below]
- Exploring Heidegger's "Clearing" and his "Space of Nothingness" [see later]
- Learning hypnosis with its experience of focus and absorption.

Walt Whitman wrote, "I am large, I contain multitudes." The Roman, Terence wrote: "Homo sum: humani nil a me alienum puto," ("I am a human: nothing human is alien to me"). I find this agonising at times... and also very useful.

Here are some ways of listening to our listening...

What are we listening **FOR**

resources / strengths / past successes / exceptions / concerns?
or
information / pathology / problems / understanding / defects?

How can we listen from different timeframes?

Past   successes / abilities?
            or
            causes / understanding?

Present   solutions / coping?
            or
            problems / suffering?

Future   possibilities / curiosity?
            or
            resignation / predictions?

Rob McNeilly

Are we listening to

The client   what they are saying, not saying, feeling,
             not feeling, doing, not doing, their concerns?
or
Ourselves   our self-talk / judgments / assessments /
             reactions?

Are we listening from our

Head   intellectual understanding of causes / logical /
          linear sequences?

Heart   emotional connection / empathy / respect?

Gut   intuitive appreciation / non-judgmental
          acceptance of legitimacy

Holistic spiritual / sacred / soul appreciation from all
          of these?

Are we listening from

Client's experience   "I can only have a hint of what
                      you mean" / "I can't understand?"
or
Our experience   "I know what you mean" / "I
                      Understand?"

Client's culture	"How are things for you?"
or	
Our culture	"This is how things should be?"
Client's beliefs	"Is this good / bad for you?"
or	
Our beliefs	"This **IS** good / bad?"

Are we listening towards

Evolving	"We can only wonder how this might be useful?"
or	
Certainty	"Now I / you / we know?"

We can now say that we are always listening FOR something, TO something, and FROM somewhere, and seeing this opens an opportunity for observation and learning. We can listen to our listening. We can listen to what we are listening for, to and from, and learn "To observe; to observe … and … to observe."

Some possible hows for you to explore:
    Notice what you are listening FOR, TO, and FROM.
    A week at a time focus on FOR, then TO, then FROM.
    What alternatives can you explore?
    What happens when you shift your listening?

BECOMING FLEXIBLE

A man living with his son, noticed that a strange horse came into his farmyard. The neighbour said, "That's good," to which the man replied, "It may be good. It may be bad." The son fell off the horse and broke his leg. The neighbour said, "That's bad," to which the man replied, "It might be bad. It might be good." The king's men came looking for soldiers to fight and the son was rejected because of his broken leg. The neighbour said, "That's good," to which the man replied, "It may be good. It may be bad." The horse escaped and the neighbour said, "That's bad," to which the man replied, "It may be bad. It may be good." The man went looking for the horse and found a whole herd of horses, which he brought home. And you can guess what the neighbour said, and how the man replied.

Heinz von Foerster said his ethical imperative was to always act to increase options and observed that the first act of a dictator is to decrease options.

There is a saying that the person with the most options controls the game and Sir William Osler goes further... "The greater the ignorance, the greater the fundamentalism."

Erickson loved puzzles as a way of softening rigidities and loved to ask how you could plant 10 trees, in 5 rows, each with 4 trees. This seems impossible until we see the option of planting them in the pattern of a five pointed star. After this, the puzzle of planting 12 trees in 6 rows each with 4 trees becomes obvious, particularly for anyone with a Jewish background.

On my second visit with Erickson, he asked the group about how many ways we could get from this room into the next. We were all starting to feel quite evolved by now and came up with a long list - falling, skipping, piggy-backing... We were quite pleased with our creativity. Erickson replied, "Yes, and you could also go outside of this room, catch a taxi to Phoenix airport, fly to Paris, Rome, Sydney, New York and then back to Phoenix, catch a taxi back here and enter the next room." None of us had considered that option, but all of us had an experience of expanding our possibilities.

He also wrote the numbers 710 on a card and asked for all the possible combinations. No-one saw OIL until the card was turned upside down and it became obvious.

When you look at these words   stand

            we

what new word becomes possible? It might be corny, but the answer is "we understand."

And once you see that,   you

           looked

becomes obvious.

 and PROM ISE

 or ever ever ever ever

can be fun to explore.

An electric train was travelling in a southerly direction at a speed of 50km/h. It was going into a headwind that was blowing directly towards the train from the south at a speed of 50 km/h. Which way did the smoke from the train go?

A rooster is sitting on the top of a house, exactly in the middle of a pitched roof that came to a sharp point. It lay an egg, which softly landed right on the point of the roof. Did the egg balance on the top of the roof or did it roll off, and if it did, which way did it roll, towards the front garden or towards the back garden?

Answers at the end of the book, if you didn't solve these yourself.

Jay Haley was asked for supervision and the student said the client had an over-enmeshed relationship with the mother, to which Haley replied, "Oh, I'd never let that be the problem!"

Lao Tzu #76.
A man is born gentle and weak.
At his death, he is hard and stiff.
Green plants are tender and filled with sap.
At their death, they are withered and dry.

Therefore, the stiff and unbending is the disciple of death.
The gentle and yielding is the disciple of life.
Thus, an army without flexibility never wins a battle.
A tree that is unbending is easily broken.
The hard and strong will fall.
The soft and weak will overcome.

Some possible hows for you to explore:

Find some books of puzzles, Sudoku, crosswords and play.

Next time you feel stuck, look for options, and when you have run out, say "or" and then find another, then say "or" again and find another. Repeat this at least 10 times.

When you find yourself doing some action in one particular way, try reversing the sequence, messing with it, leaving out bits, adding in other options... just in everyday life, such as eating a meal, travelling to a familiar place.

Do something that you've never done before... just for the fun of it.

RESTORING ADULT TRUST

Whenever we have a problem, trust is the first casualty. If we have a problem with our body, for example if we injure our leg, we become wary of using it. It's natural and useful. If there is a relationship problem, we lose trust in our partner. If we have an emotional problem, like panicking or crying, we can distrust our emotions. If we make a logical mistake, we can stop trusting our thinking.

This initial response is natural and healthy, but can become limiting if it continues beyond when it's useful. If we have a conflict, it's natural to have some fear in that experience. If we then start to fear any conflict, then this becomes a limitation, a problem.

An important question arises about restoring trust. We shouldn't trust a broken leg, but after the plaster is removed, how can we restore trust?

In a relationship betrayal, naively immediately trust again would be asking for disaster,

Fernando Flores wrote a wonderful book with Robert Solomon - "Building Trust." Books about this crucial experience are rare, and this one is a gem.

The authors distinguish naive trust, which leads to inevitable further betrayal from adult trust, where we dare to trust another while owning the consequences of betrayal. They also invite us to have the option of leading with trusting another as an expression of this adult trust instead of emphasising our trustworthiness.

A colleague told me about a client who had been fired from a series of jobs and thrown out of a series of relationships. He owned his untrustworthiness and asked for help. My colleague lent him his expensive camera with the idea that he would take some photos of some favourite places and a week later, they would develop the films together. The client was overcome with the experience of being trusted, took good care of the camera, shared the film processing a week later, which made a huge impact on his relationship with himself. My colleague ran the risk and it paid off. No-one is recommending this but it is such a wonderful possibility for us to have, as trusting someone encourages them to be trustworthy.

Flores and Solomon also write about "a window of trust" - a mood of prudence - which begins with a clearly-stated position of mutual distrust and allows for the possibility of trust developing. The end of the cold war happened though such a process. When someone has experienced violence in a relationship, simply trusting that it won't happen again is asking for further violence. The only solid possibility is to begin with an open acknowledgement of the betrayal and a conversation about how the betrayer might begin to earn back the trust of the other.

A couple wanted help because the husband had had an affair. He had stopped the affair, was completely certain about this, and although she believed him, they were having trouble becoming intimate again. We explored the genuineness of the husband and the natural reluctance of the wife, and wondered how he could

47

*begin the earn back the trust that he had damaged. She said that he would have to get rid of **that tie!** He was caught out for keeping it as a gift from the other woman. He was embarrassed and apologised and they agreed to destroy the tie together. Once he owned the restoring of trust as a process, he realised the importance of being patient, and she felt solid instead of just hoping. They destroyed the tie together and other shared events allowed the trust to develop over time.*

Some possible hows for you to explore:

Explore the legitimacy of the damage to trust in each situation and ask if the lack of trust is still relevant? If it isn't, we can find ways of letting it go. If it is still relevant, we can explore what steps and how much time will be required to restore the trust in a solid way.

Trust that a client will fulfil a commitment to perform some agreed action, and if they don't, we don't have to be disappointed or make them guilty. We trusted them, knowing that they might not keep their word.

PERSONAL DEVELOPMENT FOR THERAPISTS

"I came here with a huge open heart, like a big, sweet dog, and I still have one. But some days the only thing that can cheer me up is something bad happening to someone I hate, preferably if it went viral and the photo of the person showed hair loss and perhaps the lifelong underuse of sunscreen. My heart still leaps to see this. I often recall the New Yorker cartoon of one dog saying to the other: "It's not enough that we succeed. Cats must also fail."
Anne Lamott quoted in Maria Popova's Brain Pickings

Some therapy approaches require personal development. Anyone wanting to become a psychoanalyst must undergo analysis themselves to avoid any transference and countertransference issues.

I have noticed that a solution, client-centred approach has the possibility of avoiding many of the blindnesses that we might have as therapist, as a result of the use of questions to the client that are skewed towards an individual client's innate resourcefulness and their preferred future. The process relies more on the client's experience than the therapist's guidance and interpretation.

Even so, we therapists are also human beings. We have our own suffering, traumas, anxieties and blindnesses. If we experience a serious personal disruption, this can easily contaminate the therapy, skew our observations and even have us use the client for our benefit. Erich Fromm said that we do the work that we do, hoping that one day, one of our clients will cure us!

We can all too easily fall into the trap of taking care of others at our own expense, resulting in burnout, vicarious trauma, resignation, and hanging out for the end of the session, the day, the week, the next holiday or even retirement.

The opposite can also happen when we are impatient for a client to improve, so we don't have to feel their suffering in us. Oscar Wilde spoke about a woman that was devoted to helping her friends... and that you could tell by the haunted looks on their faces!

As with our clients, we can benefit from enjoyable activities outside the office - gardening, reading, music, walking in nature.

I have also noticed that the best form of self-care comes not only from our leisure activities, but from the satisfaction of doing good work. When we have the privilege of witnessing someone come into a session suffering, and leave relieved, peaceful, even joyful, it lifts our soul, and we can share in the relief, the peace, even the joy. This inoculates us against burnout.

Some possible hows for you to explore:

Remember to get help, like any human being, if you have a troubling problem.

Look back on your successes in your therapy work and celebrate them.

Look back on your failures and explore what learning might be useful.

Take up a hobby.

Learn Latin dancing, painting, a musical instrument, join a choir.

Do more of what you like to do.

GETTING FEEDBACK

"Statistics are like bikinis. What they reveal is fascinating but what they conceal is vital."
Paul Wayzlawick

"Am I in tune?" "Listen and you will discover."
Unknown.

To measure, or not to measure...

Years ago, there was a brand of paint that had printed on every lid "When all else fails, read the instructions."

We have all had the experience of feeling so pleased with ourselves about how a session went, only to have our pride dashed by a client's "Ho hum" response. We have also had the experience of being dissatisfied with a session, only to be shocked when a client says how transformational it was!

It turns out that we are the last person to know whether we are doing good work or not. It's like B.O. - you don't know and your friends don't tell you. It becomes obvious that the client is the final arbiter here. If the client says it was helpful, it was. If they say it wasn't, it wasn't.

But - how can we best find out?

Erickson's invitation to observe, to observe and to observe again expresses his way of keeping track of where any client was, noticing their facial expression, their body movements, their breathing, and other physiological signs. Seeing a smile, a frown, a tensing up of their fists can be so helpful. Erickson's observational skills were legendary, and he honed them over the 50 years of his professional life.

For us lesser mortals, and those of us with less experience, we can ask... "What's happening?," "How are you feeling?," "What are you beginning to discover?," "How can you maintain these changes?," "How will you know that you don't need to see me any more?" ... and so, have the opportunity to respond, adjust and realign with where the client is and where they want to go.

Some possible hows for you to explore:

For anyone wanting more precise measures of feedback, there are simple measures - Outcome Rating Scale [ORS] and Session Rating Scale [SRS] - which only take a few minutes to use, and can give a concrete measure of the client's assessment of the session and the influence in their life. They are available as a free download from

https://heartandsoulofchange.com.

They are also available along with the Child ORS and the Child SRS from http://www.pcoms.com.

There are also two programmes which track and give feedback on the results of these scales - MyOutcomes details at www.myoutcomes.com.

and also www.betteroutcomesnow.com.

SECTION 3

SOME SOURCES FOR FURTHER EXPLORATION

How many Ericksonian therapists does it take to change a light globe? It takes nineteen. One to change the light globe and eighteen to explain how they think Erickson would have done it.

MILTON ERICKSON told me personally that I should "just do good work" [hence the title of this book], rather than trying to understand his approach. I was relieved to hear this and was also left wondering how to do it.

He said that when a client comes to see you, they always bring their solution with them, although they don't know that, so have a very nice time talking with your client, helping them to find the solution that they brought that they didn't know that they brought. I was enchanted with the idea, but puzzled about how to do this.

He also said on a number of occasions that the three most important skills for us to learn are "to observe, to observe... and to observe." This gave a hint about what to do, but left the how still unanswered.

Some options began to appear when I noticed his emphasis on learning. "All problems are learnt limitations," and "All our lives, we are learning."

He embodied this principle. When I said goodbye to him on that Friday in 1980, just 10 days before he died, he was still learning within the teaching seminar I was part of, and still enjoying himself even though he was almost totally paralysed, seemingly relying on about one and a half muscles, drooling, and in considerable pain!

In many of his hypnotic sessions, he would speak about an early learning. "When you first learnt to walk...," "When you first learnt the letters of the alphabet..." inviting a revisiting of the childhood approach to learning where we were open, willing, playful as compared with our "grown-up" approach of reluctant practice and barely tolerable effort and that adults are just children grown taller.

He said that if problems can be learnt, it follows that they can be unlearnt or solutions can be learnt. We can be walking down the street and suddenly, a problem appears from nowhere for no good reason, so why can't a problem disappear into nowhere for no good reason? This sounded logical, and I liked it.

Much of his work involved reconnecting someone with some learning that they had put aside, forgotten, lost track of. He told me about a woman who rang, wanting help with her 12-year obsessive hand washing. He said he was very interested to find out what she used to do with her hands 13 years ago. What an elegant and respectful approach.

When he evoked childhood memories of learning all the letters and numbers, he spoke about the initial difficulty of consciously forming a visual mental image... which then dropped into the unconscious mind to become an unconscious learning that could be accessed any time in the future. He postulated learning in this way, beginning consciously, then becoming unconscious subsequently.

And... he also mentioned that some learnings can be direct learning in the unconscious. For example, in a history class, if someone causes a disruption, the class stops, the teacher deals with the disruption and then the class resumes. At the end of the class, everyone thinks the lesson was about history, but everyone learnt something about being respectful of others, paying attention to the teacher, focusing on the lesson.

I have found that when I am teaching, some people like to read about an approach, so they can understand the principles, others like to watch a demonstration of a session, so they can observe and incorporate some of what they see, while others like to practice and learn from their own experience. Of course, there will be some overlap, but I have found it useful to invite an exploration of how each of us learns best, so we can than allow the learning to be consistent with our own unique style.

Erickson emphasised the importance of adapting our approach to each individual, rather than expecting a client to adapt to any model of therapy we happen to like.

He championed the principle of accepting and utilising whatever any client brings and so, avoided the thankless, tedious and difficult attempt to correct any misconception that we think a client has, or to instruct them to act in ways that we claim to be wise about.

He enjoyed messing with anyone's rigid certainty, which he saw as a limitation, and instead, created confusion to soften any unhelpful certainty and open a wider range of possibilities into a preferred future. He told of a university professor at a conference that was appalled by the way Erickson ate his toast. Erickson would butter a whole slice of toast, cut it in half and then begin to eat it. The professor knew the correct way - he cut a finger of toast, buttered one end, ate it, then buttered the other end. Erickson chuckled as he said that by the end of the conference, the professor had learnt a lot about how to eat toast. I wouldn't be surprised if this professor was able to be more flexible in other areas of his life as well.

He shifted the predominant time orientation from understand past causes, from merely being present, and towards future possibilities. He wrote that in his experience, people came to therapy not primarily because of the unchangeable past, but because of some discontent in the present and a desire to better their future.

And, he did a lot more than this, as the masses of books written about him demonstrate.

MARTIN HEIDEGGER wrote about "the clearing" as an experience where we can become so connected with our surroundings - nature, a book, a film... or a client - that we merge and disappear into the totality, connecting at a profound level, and losing our self-awareness. Our judgements also disappear, so we can be at one with whatever is there and find ourselves in a sacred space, one which is profoundly healing.

He wrote of the experience of walking in a forest, and suddenly "seeing" the forest as the forest. The forest appears out of the background, where we were previously unaware of it. We may have been thinking about something, feeling hungry, tired, excited, but unaware of the forest with our attention elsewhere. When we "see" the forest, we connect with it in a novel and holistic way.

In "the clearing" we disappear as an observer, and there is nothing between us and the forest. It is as if we, as observers, are not there. We are so present that we merge with the forest, and it doesn't make sense to speak of us or the forest – we and the forest become "we-in-the-forest" to follow Heidegger's "being-in-the-world." We become transparent.

How can we connect with each client's clearing?

Following Erickson's invitation "to observe, to observe, and to observe," we can find ourselves naturally letting go of our judgements, reactions and opinions about the client, and become curious and listen to who they are, what is important to them, what they care about, how they make their own sense of their experience. This encourages a shift in our focus away from us and our competence and towards the client and their experience.

Martin Heidegger spoke of "the always, already listening that we are," which allows us to have a glimpse of how we are automatically ready to listen, look out for, anticipate from our own particular perspective. Pessimists listen for problems and expect them; optimists listen for benefits and expect them; car mechanics listen for defects; bird watchers listen for birds. In this context, we are saying that listening is not just a function of our ears, but includes our eyes, nose, and other senses, as well as remembered and anticipated experiences, and opens a rich area of exploration.

He also claims that human beings are concerned beings, are oriented towards the world in a non-random manner, always act from a concern, always taking care of some concern. He uses the word "concern" to point to something we care about, something that we value, or hold as important to us. This allows us to explore concerns - to listen for them in each individual.

He also wrote about "the space of nothingness" as an experience that complements "the clearing." Here it is, as if everything around us disappears and all there is, is us. There is no forest, there is only us.

Rafael Echeverria summarised the clearing as total connection with no observer and the space of nothingness as total disconnection with nothing but the observer.

TIMOTHY GALLWEY wrote The Inner Game of Tennis in 1974 and when I first read it, it reminded me of Milton Erickson's approach.

In his introduction, Gallwey writes, "There is a far more natural and effective process for learning and doing almost anything than most of us realize. It is similar to the process we all used, but soon forgot, as we learnt to walk and talk. It uses the intuitive capabilities of the mind... All that is needed is to *un*learn those habits which interfere with it and then to just *let it happen*."

In parallel to Erickson's recommendation to "trust your unconscious mind," Gallwey writes about Self 1 [ego, judging, controlling, the conscious mind] and Self 2 [letting, experiencing, learning, imaging, the unconscious mind] and champions the process of putting judgements [good and bad] aside and being present to "what is," of "nonjudgemental awareness." He gives examples of how people he coached were able to correct faults in their game - faults that they were aware of and had previously been unable to correct. This is achieved by quieting Self 1, and trusting Self 2.

Interestingly he cautions against encouraging "positive" outcomes, claiming that they interfere with learning naturally. Instead, he encourages "nonjudgemental observation of change and results," creating more freedom and greater depth of learning.

"The more awareness one can bring to bear on any action, the more feedback one gets from experience, and the more naturally one learns the technique that feels best and works best for any given player at any given stage of development. Bottom line: there is no substitute for learning from experience."

"The Inner Game way of learning is a return towards this childlike way."

"It would be useful for all tennis players to undergo some "sensitivity training with their bodies" [p89] and invites attending to different senses - watching the ball and its trajectory, listening to the sound of the ball as it bounces and connects with the racket, attending the feel of the racket, the rhythm of the play, and is reminiscent of Fritz Perls' invitation to "lose your mind and come to your senses," of Fernando Flores emphasising increasing sensitivities and Erickson's invitation "to observe, to observe, and to observe." This focus on sensing is one more way Gallwey offers to get Self 1 out of the way by giving it something to focus on so that Self 2 can do what it knows best.

Gallwey shares how he has learnt to facilitate the Self 2 experience. He has found that "it comes in its own timing, when I am ready for it - humble, respectful, not expecting it, somehow placing myself lower than it, not higher. Then when the moment is right, it comes, and I can enjoy the absence of Self 1 thought and the presence of joy."

Rob McNeilly

FERNANDO FLORES offers a beautifully refreshing insight into the experience of learning when he writes with Charles Spinosa and Hubert L Dreyfus in Disclosing New Worlds, *"This book, then, is attempting to develop sensitivities, not knowledge. Once one has a sensitivity to something such as good food, decency, certain kinds of beauty, or even the pleasures of hiking, one is already on the path of refining and developing that sensitivity. One sees food, decent behavior, beauty, and hiking trails in a new light. They draw one to them in a way they did not before. As one is drawn, time and time again, one then continuously develops one's skills for dealing with what one is sensitive to."*

In emphasising "sensitivities," he is inviting us to be immersed in an activity and through this immersion, to allow our learning to happen organically, not linearly, intellectually or intentionally.

Later he writes, *"When people are captivated by an unusual game, for example, they just play and play, losing all sense of their surroundings, while working at the game with complete absorption and hypersensitivity but **not, and this is important to remember, with the curiosity of reflective thought."*** [emphasis mine] and again champions learning through increased sensitivity instead the intellectual process of reflective thought.

Linking learning sensitivities to learning therapy brings new opportunities to facilitate learning.

How we are relating to learning is changing. Until recently, we thought of knowing as acquiring information, arranging or computing that information to create an understanding or a model of understanding that we could then act on - something like making a map of an area of country and then using the map to find our way around.

It is crucial to distinguish education from teaching here. Education – from the Latin "educare" – to draw out - is very different from the imparting of information, requiring that it be taken in, or teaching, which requires compliance with some external protocol. Imparting information and teaching require a passivity by the student, and bring a mood of fear with a concern for control.

Education is a creative experience requiring active participation by the student, and brings a mood of legitimacy, curiosity, and openness.

HUMBERTO MATURANA claimed that his friend, Heinz von Foerster, was a magician. Together, they said that "Magic is the art of dealing with things you don't understand by grasping coherences, which allow you to deal with them even without understanding," i.e. without reference to intellectual reflective thought.

He also wrote in "Something Beyond Greatness," "We human beings are fundamentally loving beings. Something happens when you see the legitimacy of the other. Love just sees, and then you act according to what you see. If you let the other be, the other will appear in their legitimacy and you will act accordingly," and also, "What an observer sees as greatness is simply acting in candour and innocence, doing what the present moment calls for. It is the candour and innocence of "letting be," the candour and innocence of forgetting greatness."

For me, this emphasis is not trivial. It invites and allows a letting go of understanding, quantifying, explaining, theorising, and instead, we can experience! This can require practice or learning, but no chore, simply learning to have a natural self-expression in response to what is seen to be there.

In their book "The Tree of Knowledge," he and Varela write about structural determinism as a way of recognising that any structure can only do what its structure will allow. A washing machine can't be expected to make toast, and a toaster can't be expected to wash clothes. When we apply this to human dilemmas, it can be such a relief to recognise that when a client has a problem, simply requiring that they stop it and have a solution instead simply doesn't make sense. It's only when their structure has changed that a new action becomes possible.

They also claim that the central nervous system is a closed system with no "holes" for anything to enter. All we can do is to be with a client, do something, invite something, to initiate a perturbation within the client and only discover what that will be after it has happened. We cannot introduce something new into another person, only create a perturbation and then respond to that.

This disqualifies any idea of instructing, fixing or changing another in any predetermined way, and evidences the importance of listening, accepting, being flexible, etc. - all the skills we explored earlier in this book.

WERNER ERHARD founded EST in the 80s which evolved into The Forum and then into The Landmark Forum. Mentioning his name often provokes a strong reaction and I have yet to hear a neutral response from anyone who has heard about him. People love him or hate him.

On reading his name here, some readers might decide to throw this book into the flames and write me off as a cult member. More than one person has decided not to join my teaching programme after reading his name as part of my background.

A number of eminent therapists have also expressed their appreciation of his contribution to their person, their life and their work.

He brings an unlikely mix of Eastern mysticism, possibly from his one-time neighbour, Allan Watts, also Stoicism, Gestalt Therapy, Provocative Therapy and Flores' language action paradigm.

In programmes designed by him, I have been touched and moved by the privilege of seeing people break through limiting beliefs and stories, and step into a fuller expression of who they are and what they are up to, and instead of being caught in personal dramas, make extraordinary contributions, including peace talks in Ireland.

I continue to be grateful to this man's contribution to me from 1985 and continuing into my future.

One of the major contributions is the deconstruction of a problem experience into a past event and the story that follows and keeps the past alive. The process, according to this approach goes:

Something happens.
We make up a story.
We look for evidence to back up the story.
We forget we made up the story.
Then the story lives us.

Another major contribution is the active process of creating a possibility, literally out of nothing. This act of declaring reveals the hidden side of language as the source of action, not merely description. I have had numerous personal emergings that I attribute directly to this approach, including writing this and other books.

These opportunities can allow for an unlearning of some unwanted experiences and the creation of something preferable - a transformation from problem and stuckness into solution and possibilities. I have found this experience to be a useful development process for therapists.

Rob McNeilly

Lao Tzu

If I were to be sent to a desert island and be allowed one book, I'd choose Tao te Ching. If I were allowed two books, I'd choose two copies of the Tao. The mood of this timeless poetry has been a reliable source of peace and inspiration for me over the last 40 years. The text speaks to perennial human dilemmas and is appreciated across all cultures.

1

The Tao that can be told is not the eternal Tao.

The name that can be named is not the eternal name.

The nameless is the beginning of heaven and earth.

The named is the mother of ten thousand things.

Ever desireless, one can see the mystery.

Ever desiring, one can see the manifestations.

These two spring from the same source but differ in name;

this appears as darkness.

Darkness within darkness.

The gate to all mystery.

15

The ancient masters were subtle, mysterious, profound, responsive.

The depth of their knowledge is unfathomable.

Because it is unfathomable, all we can do is describe their appearance.

Watchful, like men crossing a winter stream.

Alert, like men aware of danger.

Courteous, like visiting guests.

Yielding, like ice about to melt.

Simple, like uncarved blocks of wood.

Hollow, like caves.

Opaque, like muddy pools.

Who can wait quietly while the mud settles?

Who can remain still until the moment of action?

Observers of the Tao do not seek fulfilment.

Not seeking fulfilment, they are not swayed by desire for change.

32.

The Tao is forever undefined.

....

Tao in the world is like a river flowing home to the sea.

48.

In the pursuit of learning, every day something is acquired.

In the pursuit of Tao, every day something is dropped.

Less and less is done

Until non-action is achieved.

When nothing is done, nothing is left undone.

The world is ruled by letting things take their course.

It cannot be ruled by interfering.

56.

Those who know do not talk.

Those who talk do not know.

....

MEDITATION

There are many meditation practices available and mindfulness is the latest trend.

Mindfulness meditation is derived from an ancient Buddhist practice and has been simplified, some say disrespectfully, so it is more easily accessible to our contemporary western lifestyle.

There are many variations, but all invite a focus - on the breath, or anything that can be sensed - a sound, an object, a taste, a sensation - with the practice of bringing the focus back any time it wanders off.

My friend Peter Thorneycroft has produced a series of audio experiences that don't require any effort, just a willingness to listen through stereo earphones. I have noticed my personal benefit of listening to these regularly.

ZEN

For me the simplicity of Zen is its most beautiful contribution and at the same time, the most challenging. We humans like to complicate experiences into problems, and Zen offers a way back to the simple uncluttered source, to the Taoist "uncarved block."

"When Banzan was walking through a market he overheard a conversation between a butcher and his customer.

"Give me the best piece of meat you have," said the customer.

"Everything in my shop is the best," replied the butcher.

"You cannot find here any piece of meat that is not the best."

At these words Banzan became enlightened." Everything is Best. Zen Flesh, Zen Bones.

When a Zen monk's hut burnt down, he said he now had an uninterrupted view of the moon! How elegant!

THE STOICS

The Stoic attitude begins with recognising the possibility of bad things happening, while holding the certainty that we can accept them with equanimity.

Seneca wrote "When a shipwreck was reported and he heard that all his possessions had sunk, our founder Zeno said, "Fortune bids me be a less encumbered philosopher."

When Seneca was told that all his family had been killed, he replied that all his goods were with him. Anything that could be taken from him was not part of him.

This radical acceptance is a direct path to peace for anyone willing to take it.

One of my favourite sayings is that experience is a given and suffering is always an option. I wonder how many times I will need to say this before I have learnt the experience. Will I manage it in this lifetime? And... I find it helpful to be reminded.

THE MULLA NASRUDIN

The Mulla, popular in Turkey as a whimsical expression of the Sufi tradition, was popularised in the west by Idre Shah, and had a way of stating the obvious in a quirky way so we can see the obviousness and also the absurdity of our human condition.

Nasrudin was on his hands and knees under a street light and his neighbour asks what he was doing. "I'm looking for my house key," he replied. The neighbour joined him looking and when after some time, they hadn't found it, he asked if the Mulla was certain he'd dropped the key here. Nasrudin replied that he'd actually dropped the key over there. The puzzled neighbour asked why they were looking here. Nasrudin replied, "The light's better over here."

The same neighbour asked to borrow Nasrudin's donkey. Nasrudin said he could, except that he'd lent the donkey to someone else. Just then the donkey brayed from the back of the house. When the neighbour challenged Nasrudin, he replied, "Anyone who takes my donkey's word over mine doesn't deserve to be leant a donkey."

The long suffering neighbour asked to borrow Nasrudin's clothes line. Nasrudin said he couldn't because he was drying flour on it. The neighbour said that it must be difficult to dry flour on a clothes line to which The Mulla replied, "It's not at all difficult when you don't want to lend your clothes line."

These mystics offer an antidote to the flatland mood of our contemporary intellectual society, and so to a richer human experience.

SERENDIPITY

When I look back on the major influence in my life, I am amazed at my good fortune in being offered so many unexpected opportunities.

When I was in a personal crisis many years ago, I sought help from Ainslie Meares, a traditionally trained psychiatrist in Melbourne Australia where I was living, and this led to me exploring hypnosis.

I learnt a traditional authoritative approach to hypnosis, which was somewhat effective, but didn't sit well with me with its power issues. However, when I was at an international conference and heard about Milton Erickson for the first time and saw Herbert Lustig's "The Artistry of Milton H Erickson" and fell in love with Erickson and his approach. This led to me spending time with him in the last few years of his life and resulted in an invitation from Jeffrey Zeig to contribute to the First International Conference on the Ericksonian Approaches to Hypnosis and Psychotherapy in Phoenix in 1980, and to a number of similar conferences in the 35 years since.

When Jeffrey Zeig needed some organisational help for a workshop in Melbourne, Australia, he asked me, and this led to me organising other teaching visits by Joseph Barber, Michael Yapko, Stephen Lankton and Bill O'Hanlon over the following decade or so.

Other Australian therapist got to know about me as a result and I was able to begin a teaching career running workshops around Australia, and then Singapore, Denmark, Japan, Finland, Brazil, UK and Czech Republic.

I was introduced to the online environment by Bill O'Hanlon and now my teaching is increasingly online, which is a wonderful experience.

How could anyone have designed such a journey?

Serendipity offers us opportunities, and if we have the eyes to see them, we have the option of following, for which I continue to be grateful.

ANSWERS TO THE PUZZLES:

PROM ISE   broken promise

ever ever ever ever   four [for] ever

An electric train has no smoke.

Roosters don't lay eggs.

REFERENCES

Better Outcomes Now
http://www.betteroutcomesnow.com

Echeverria, Rafael. (1993) *El Buho De Minerva*. Santiago, Chile: Dolemen Ediciones

Furman, Ben (2004) *Kids' Skills - Playful and practical solution-finding with children*. Bendigo, Australia: St Luke's Innovative Resources

Gallwey, W. Timothy. (1974) *The Inner Game of Tennis*. New York, New York: Random House.

Haley, Jay. (1967) *Advanced Techniques of Hypnosis and Therapy, Selected Papers of Milton H Erickson MD*. New York, New York: Grune & Stratton

Leslie, Paul J.. (2014) *Low Country Shamanism, An Exploration of the Magical and Healing Practices of the Coastal Carolinas and Georgia*. USA: Path Notes Press.

Maturana, Humberto R. and Varela, Francisco J. (1988) *The Tree of Knowledge. The biological Roots of Human Understanding.* Boston: Shambala Publications, Inc.

MyOutcomes www.myoutcomes.com.

ORS & SRS https://heartandsoulofchange.com. and http://www.pcoms.com.

Popova, Maria. (16th April, 2017) *Brain Pickings:* https://www.brainpickings.org

Reps, P. [compiled] (1971) *Zen Flesh, Zen Bones.* Middlesex, England: Penguin Books

Seneca *On Tranquility of mind. London, England:* Penguin Books Ltd

Shah, Idre. *The Subtleties of the Inimitable Mulla Nasrudin. London, UK:* Octagon Press

Solomon, Robert C. and Flores, Fernando. (2001) *Building Trust in Business, Politics, Relationships, and Life.* New York, New York: Oxford University Press.

Spinosa, Charles, and Flores, Fernando and Dreyfus, Hubert L.. (1997) *Disclosing New Worlds*. Cambridge, Massachusetts, and London, England: MIT Press.

Thorneycroft, Peter W.. http://www.peterthorneycroft.com

Tzu, Lao. Translated by Feng, Gia-Fu and English, Jane (1972) *Tao Te Ching*. New York, New York: Vantage Books.

About The Author

Robert McNeilly was in general medical practice for 10 years, conducted a private hypnotherapy practice for 35 years, and after meeting Milton H Erickson in USA, began teaching diploma courses in counselling and hypnosis with a solution orientation to interested health workers nationally and internationally.

He has authored another 5 books - "Healing with Words" with Jenny Brown and "Healing the Whole Person" published by Wiley, republished as "Doing Change - conversations for moving on" by St Luke's Innovative Resources. With Tandava Press Creating Connections Vol 1 & 2 and Learning Hypnosis. He has also published a number of eBooks with Amazon Kindle.

Robert B McNeilly MBBS
Director, The Centre of Effective Therapy
Co-director, The Milton H Erickson Institute of Tasmania
191 Campbell Street
Hobart TAS 7000
Australia
email rob@cet.net.au
www.cet.net.au

NOTES

NOTES

NOTES

NOTES

NOTES

NOTES

NOTES

NOTES

www.ingramcontent.com/pod-product-compliance
Lightning Source LLC
Chambersburg PA
CBHW030025290326
41934CB00005B/494